Joe Biden

A Little Golden Book® Biography

By Shana Corey
Illustrated by Lauren Gallegos

🌸 A GOLDEN BOOK • NEW YORK

rhcbooks.com
Educators and librarians, for a variety of teaching tools, visit us at RHTeachersLibrarians.com
Library of Congress Control Number: 2021932626
ISBN 978-0-593-47938-4 (trade) — ISBN 978-0-593-47939-1 (ebook)
Printed in the United States of America
10 9 8 7 6 5 4 3 2

Joe Biden is the 46th president of the United States of America.

Joe was born in Scranton, Pennyslvania, in 1942. He and his friends played baseball and football. They rode bikes and went to the movies. Joe was a natural leader and was always up for a challenge. He climbed flagpoles and swung high on ropes. Joe knew he could do big things.

Joe's family was Catholic. On Sundays, they went to church. Then they'd go back to Joe's grandpop's house and talk about news and politics. Listening to his family and to the nuns at school, Joe learned how important it is to treat all people with dignity and respect.

"I learned... no one was better than me. But I was no better than anybody else."

When Joe was ten, his family moved to Delaware. Some things, like sports, came easily to Joe. But other things, like reading out loud in class, were harder. Joe had a stutter that made him stumble over his words.

Sometimes kids made fun of him.
Sometimes even grown-ups made fun of him.

Joe's father told him it doesn't matter how many times you get knocked down. What matters is that you get back up. So whenever Joe stumbled, he made sure to get back up and keep trying.

Joe memorized paragraphs he would have to read out loud in class. He practiced at a mirror. Talking in front of people wasn't easy, but Joe kept working on it.

Joe dreamed of going to a fancy Catholic high school, but his family couldn't afford it. He spent the summer before his freshman year working for the school to help pay his tuition. He washed windows and painted fences and weeded the garden. And when school started, Joe took his place with the other students.

The students were required to give a speech at a big assembly. Joe was told he didn't have to because of his stutter, but he didn't want to be treated differently. So he kept practicing and practicing. And in his sophomore year, he gave the speech. It was one of Joe's proudest moments.

As Joe grew up, he became more and more interested in politics. He went to college and studied politics and history. Then he went to law school. Joe admired leaders like Martin Luther King Jr. and John F. Kennedy, who were fighting for change. He remembered the talks around his grandfather's table. He believed that politics could make people's lives better—and he wanted to help.

When Joe was 29 years old, he decided to run for the United States Senate. There are just 100 senators, two from each state, and it's their job to help make laws. Joe's sister was his campaign manager. Joe was married now, and his wife and the rest of his family helped, too. Joe had to speak to people all over Delaware to ask for their vote. It wasn't easy, but he was starting to like public speaking. Joe won the election and became one of the youngest people ever elected to the Senate!

Joe still had struggles in his life. His wife
and their baby daughter died in a car accident.
Sometimes he was sad. Sometimes he was angry.
But no matter how hard things were, Joe managed
to get back up and keep going.

Joe was a leader in the Senate. He eventually fell in love and got married again. His wife, Jill, was a teacher. Every day, Joe took the train from Washington, DC, back home to his family in Delaware. Joe served as Delaware's senator for 36 years—the longest in Delaware's history.

In 2008, Barack Obama asked Joe to be his vice president. Joe said yes. For eight years, Joe was Obama's vice president—and his friend.

President Obama trusted him. Joe traveled all over the world representing the United States. He worked to bring American troops home from overseas. And he helped create jobs. President Obama called Joe the best vice president America has ever had and awarded him the Presidential Medal of Freedom.

Joe Biden wasn't done facing big challenges. In 2019, he decided to run for president of the United States. Joe chose Kamala Harris, a senator from California, to be his vice president.

There had never been a female or a Black or an Asian vice president before. Joe knew that he and Kamala could do big things and help make Americans' lives better.

On Election Day in 2020, Americans went to the polls to make their voices heard. There was a new virus in the world, so many voted by mail. And when the votes were counted, Joe Biden and Kamala Harris won! They got 81 million votes—more than any presidential candidate had ever gotten before.

On January 20, 2021, Joe Biden became the 46th president of the United States. He stood proudly and spoke to the entire country. He talked about the values his family had taught him— like decency and dignity—that he thought could help everyone. And he asked Americans to work together. "The American story depends not on any one of us . . . but on all of us," he said. "We can do great things."

Joe Biden is part of the American story. He always has been, even as a kid playing ball and riding his bike. We are all part of the American story. And we can do big things—great things, too—just like Joe!